WEIRDEST Animals

Coconut Crabs

Big Buddy Books

An Imprint of Abdo Publishing
abdopublishing.com

Marcia Zappa

abdopublishing.com

Published by Abdo Publishing, a division of ABDO, PO Box 398166, Minneapolis, Minnesota 55439. Copyright © 2016 by Abdo Consulting Group, Inc. International copyrights reserved in all countries. No part of this book may be reproduced in any form without written permission from the publisher. Big Buddy Books™ is a trademark and logo of Abdo Publishing.

Printed in the United States of America, North Mankato, Minnesota.
042015
092015

Cover Photos: Glow Images; Shutterstock.com.
Interior Photos: Ingo Arndt/Minden Pictures (p. 29); ©Stephen Belcher/Minden Pictures (p. 5); Tui De Roy/ Minden Pictures (p. 15); ©Jean-Paul Ferrero/AUSCAPE (p. 23); altrendo travel/Getty Images (p. 27); Pete Atkinson/Getty Images (p. 11); Stephen Belcher/Minden Pictures/Getty Images (p. 21); Martin Harvey/ Getty Images (p. 17); Michele Westmorland/Getty Images (p. 7); Alexander Yates/Getty Images (p. 25); Minden Pictures/AP Images (p. 30); Shutterstock.com (pp. 9, 19).

Coordinating Series Editor: Rochelle Baltzer
Contributing Editors: Megan M. Gunderson, Bridget O'Brien, Sarah Tieck
Graphic Design: Adam Craven

Library of Congress Cataloging-in-Publication Data

Zappa, Marcia, 1985- author.
  Coconut crabs / Marcia Zappa.
    pages cm. -- (World's weirdest animals)
  ISBN 978-1-62403-772-6
1. Coconut crab--Juvenile literature. I. Title.
  QL444.M338Z37 2016
  595.3'8--dc23
                         2015004766

Contents

Wildly Weird!

The world is full of weird, wonderful animals. Coconut crabs are the largest land crabs. And, they have an unusual habit. They use their strong claws to steal things. These features make coconut crabs wildly weird!

An adult coconut crab can measure up to three feet (1 m) from leg tip to leg tip. It can weigh up to about nine pounds (4 kg).

Bold Bodies

Coconut crabs are invertebrates (ihn-VUHR-tuh-bruhts). They don't have skeletons inside their bodies. Instead, adult coconut crabs have hard outer shells called exoskeletons.

Adult coconut crabs vary in color. They may be white, orange, red, purple, blue, or brown. Some are speckled, striped, or a mix of colors.

Did You Know?

Coconut crabs are a type of hermit crab. Most hermit crabs don't grow exoskeletons. Instead, they use empty shells to protect their soft abdomens.

Coconut crabs grow their own hard outer shells. That's why they can grow much larger than other crabs!

A coconut crab has five pairs of legs. The first pair has large claws. These are used to get food and carry objects. The middle three pairs are used to walk. The last pair is used to keep the **gills** wet.

A coconut crab has two red eyes that stick up off its head. It has two pairs of antennae (an-TEH-nee). One pair helps it smell. The other helps it feel its surroundings. Bristles on the claws also help the coconut crab feel.

Did You Know?

Coconut crabs breathe through special gills. Soft skin around the gills must be kept wet. But even though they have gills, adult coconut crabs are land animals. They will drown if underwater too long.

EYE

ANTENNA

LEG

CLAW

9

Thief!

Coconut crabs are also called robber crabs. They are known to carry off items people leave lying around.

Coconut crabs may steal food or shoes. They will also steal silverware, pots and pans, and many other things they get their claws on!

A coconut crab's claws can lift up to 62 pounds (28 kg)!

Where in the World?

Coconut crabs live on **tropical** islands in the Pacific and Indian Oceans. Their main **habitat** is sandy or rocky shores. But, they can also be found as far as 3.7 miles (6 km) inland.

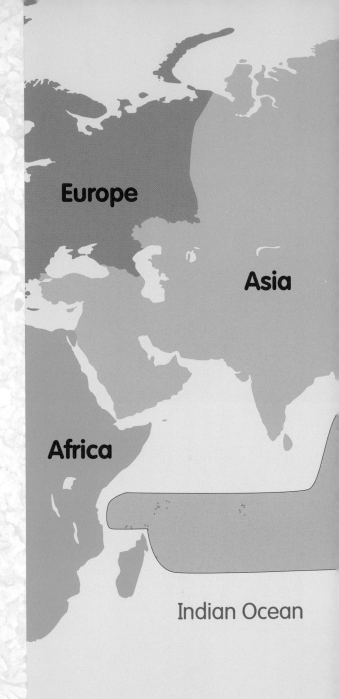

Europe

Asia

Africa

Indian Ocean

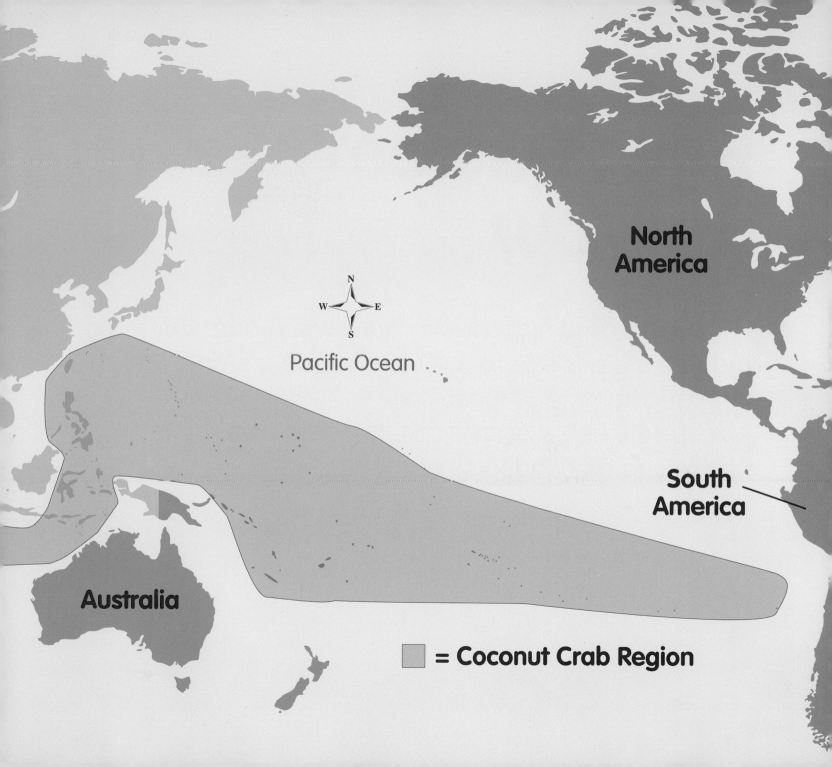

North America

South America

Pacific Ocean

Australia

= Coconut Crab Region

Home Sweet Burrow

Adult coconut crabs live in **burrows**. A burrow may be a crack in a rock. Or, it may be a small hole dug in sand or loose soil.

A burrow helps keep a coconut crab safe. And, it can be used to store food.

Coconut crabs usually live alone. But sometimes, two crabs share a burrow.

A Crab's Life

Coconut crabs are most active at night. During the day, they hide in their **burrows**. This keeps them from drying out in the sun.

Hiding in burrows also helps coconut crabs stay safe from **predators**. Pigs, rats, and monkeys hunt young crabs. And, people catch adult crabs to eat.

At night, coconut crabs can often be found in trees. Their long legs make them good climbers.

Feeding Time

Coconut crabs are omnivores (AHM-nih-vawrs). That means they eat both plants and animals. They often eat fruits and seeds. They also eat other crabs and the remains of dead animals.

Coconut crabs usually search for food at night. They use their strong sense of smell to find food. Sometimes, they climb trees to cut down fruits and seeds. They also use their powerful claws to crack open hard foods, such as other crabs.

Coconut crabs need calcium to make their exoskeletons strong. To get calcium, they eat shells shed by other crabs (*below*). And, they eat their own exoskeletons after shedding!

Crazy for Coconuts

Coconut crabs were named for one of their favorite foods, the coconut. Often, they eat coconuts that have fallen to the ground and split open.

Other times, these crabs use their claws to pull off a coconut's hairs. They poke a weak spot to break it open. Then, they can eat the fruit inside!

Did You Know?

Coconut crabs bring large pieces of food to their burrows to store for later.

It is hard work for a coconut crab to pull off a coconut's hairs. Sometimes, two or more crabs work together at this job.

Life Cycle

Coconut crabs **mate** on land. The mother lays thousands of eggs. She carries them beneath her **abdomen**.

When the eggs are ready to **hatch**, the mother goes to the ocean. There, she lets go of her eggs. The eggs hatch into **larvae**. They live in the water and eat tiny sea plankton.

Did You Know?

Female coconut crabs have special body parts called pleopods that hold their eggs.

Coconut crab mothers can lay more than 50,000 eggs at a time!

Growing Up

A coconut crab **larva** lives in the ocean for three to four weeks. Its body changes as it grows. It finds an empty shell to live in. This keeps it safe.

Before long, the young crab crawls onto the shore. It continues to grow and change. In time, it digs a **burrow**. After two to three years, it grows a hard exoskeleton over its **abdomen**.

When a young coconut crab gets too big for its shell, it finds a bigger one.

To continue growing, an older coconut crab molts. This means it **sheds** its exoskeleton. Then it grows a new, larger one.

A coconut crab continues to molt and grow year after year. Most coconut crabs reach their full size after about 40 years.

Did You Know?

Coconut crabs molt in the safety of their burrows.

Molting can take more than three weeks. Large crabs take longer to molt than small crabs.

World Wide Weird

On some islands, coconut crabs are common. But on others, there are not many left. Much of their **habitat** has been destroyed as people visit and move there. And, some people collect too many coconut crabs to eat.

It is important to know how our actions affect wild animals. With care, we can keep weird, wonderful animals such as coconut crabs around for years to come.

In some places, there are laws about when people can collect coconut crabs. And, laws say how big a coconut crab must be for it to be taken.

FAST FACTS ABOUT:
Coconut Crabs

Animal Type – invertebrate

Size – up to 3 feet (1 m) from leg tip to leg tip

Weight – up to about 9 pounds (4 kg)

Habitat – rocky and sandy shores of islands in the Pacific and Indian Oceans

Diet – fruits, seeds, other crabs, and the remains of dead animals

What makes the coconut crab wildly weird?

It is the largest known land crab in the world, and it steals unusual objects!

Glossary

abdomen (AB-duh-muhn) the rear part of a crab's body.

burrow an animal's underground home.

gill an organ that helps an animal breathe by getting oxygen from water.

habitat a place where a living thing is naturally found.

hatch to be born from an egg.

larva (LAHR-vuh) the early form of an animal, such as a crab, that must change before it is in adult form.

mate to join as a couple in order to reproduce, or have babies.

predator a person or animal that hunts and kills animals for food.

shed to cast aside or lose as part of a natural process of life.

tropical of or relating to parts of the world where temperatures are warm and the air is moist all the time.

Websites

To learn more about World's Weirdest Animals, visit **booklinks.abdopublishing.com**. These links are routinely monitored and updated to provide the most current information available.

Index